INSPIRATIONAL

Picture Quotes

About

GRATITUDE

GABI RUPP

lean jumpstart

To: ....

From: ....

Dear reader,
this is a book to always carry with you
and cherish, to be there whenever you need
to be uplifted. Enjoy insightful, and famous
quotes about gratitude and thankfulness.
These carefully selected quotations will
help inspire you and focus your energy on
what to appreciate in your life.
Thank you and feel the power of gratitude!

Gabi Rupp

Nature's beauty is
a gift that cultivates
APPRECIATION
and gratitude

LOUIE SCHWARTZBERG

The roots of all goodness
lie in the soil of appreciation
for goodness.
~Dalai Lama

As we express our gratitude,
we must never forget
that the highest appreciation
is not to utter words,
but to live by them.
~John F. Kennedy

There are slavish souls who carry their
appreciation for favors done them so far
that they strangle themselves
with the rope of gratitude.
~Friedrich Nietzsche

Appreciation

Prayer

One single grateful thought
raised to heaven
is the most perfect prayer.
~G. E. Lessing

Thank you' is the best prayer
that anyone could say.
I say that one a lot.
Thank you expresses
extreme gratitude,
humility, understanding.
~Alice Walker

If the only prayer you said
in your whole life was,
"thank you,"
that would suffice.
~Meister Eckhart

Tänan Mālō

Néa'eše

どうも

Köszi 唔該 ਸ਼ੁਕਰੀਆ

Dank u   Faleminderit Kiitos

多謝   Qagaasakuq Ahxéhee

Merci   Obrigado Māuruuru

Paldies   감사합니다   Děkoju

Mersi გმადლობთ   Terima kasih

Ευχαριστώ   Vielen Dank

Dziękuję   Merci beaucoup Qujanaq   Рахмат

謝謝   благодаря   Asante

Thank you

Ngiyabonga

Danke schön

Muchas gracias

Hvala धन्यवाद   Мулцумеск

Gracias   Danke   Grazie   Děkuju

Takk   Tack   Спасибо

Thanks   Дзякуй

Hohóu   Many thanks

Хвала Mahalo

Pilámaya

Ďakujem Teşekkürle

Uankon

Thankfulness
is the beginning of gratitude.
Gratitude
is the completion of thankfulness.
Thankfulness may consist
merely of words.
Gratitude is shown in acts.
~Henri Frederic Amiel

Often people ask how I manage
to be happy despite having
no arms and no legs.
The quick answer is that I have a choice.
I can be angry about not having limbs, or
I can be thankful that I have a purpose.
I chose gratitude.
~Nick Vujicic

Gratitude is our most direct line to God
and the angels. If we take the time,
no matter how crazy and troubled
we feel, we can find something
to be thankful for.
~Terry Lynn Taylor

Gratitude
is the most
exquisite form
of courtesy.
~Jacques
Maritain

Gratitude
is not only the
greatest of virtues,
but the parent
of all the others.
~Marcus Tullius Cicero

Feeling gratitude
isn't born in us –
it's something
we are taught,
and in turn,
we teach
our children.
~Joyce Brothers

Virtue

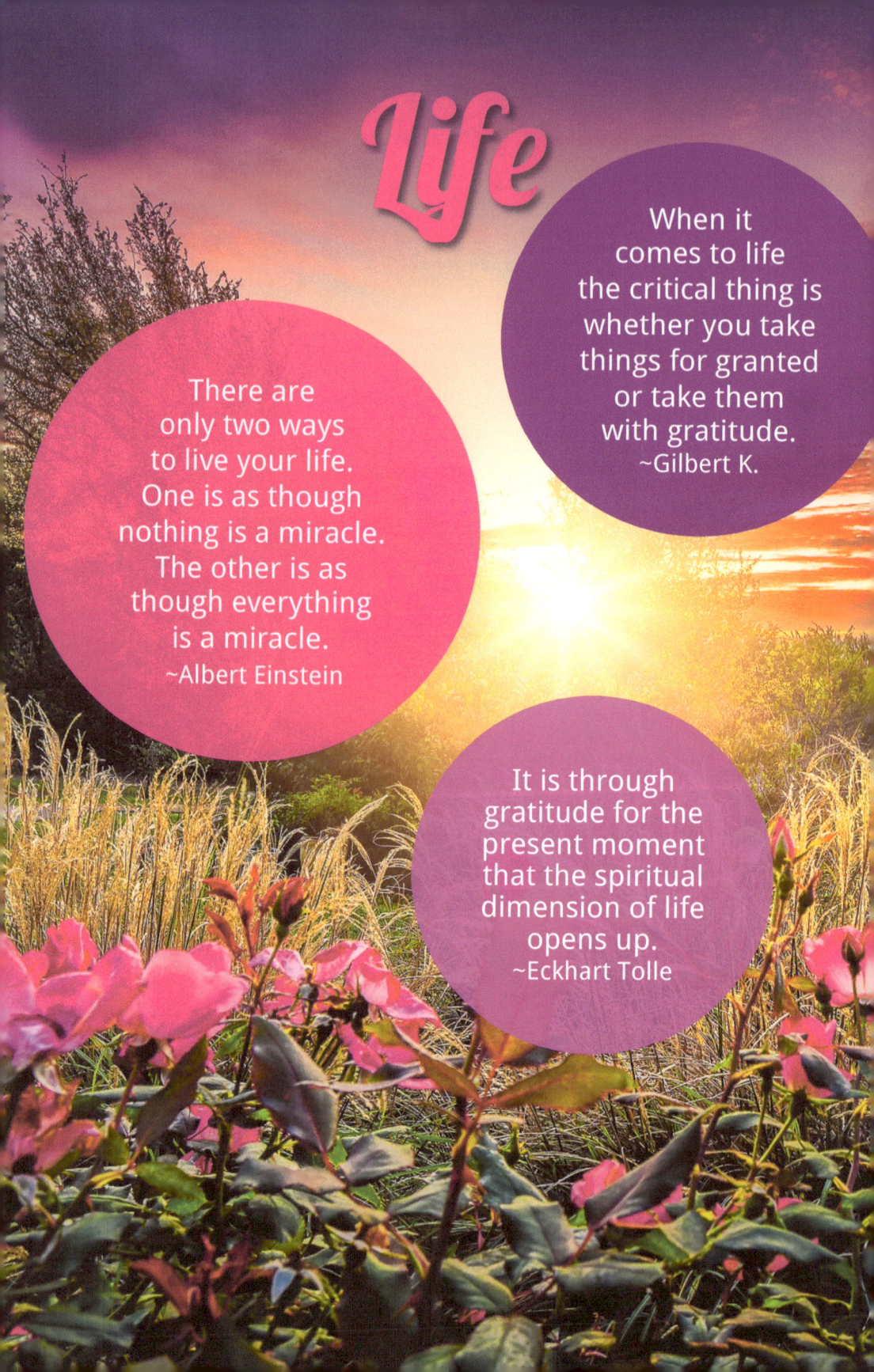

Life

When it comes to life the critical thing is whether you take things for granted or take them with gratitude.
~Gilbert K.

There are only two ways to live your life. One is as though nothing is a miracle. The other is as though everything is a miracle.
~Albert Einstein

It is through gratitude for the present moment that the spiritual dimension of life opens up.
~Eckhart Tolle

To speak
gratitude is courteous
and pleasant,
to enact gratitude
is generous and noble,
but to live gratitude
is to touch heaven.
~Johannes A. Gaertner

For it is in
GIVING
that we receive

FRANCIS OF ASSISI

Two kinds
of gratitude:
the sudden
kind we feel
for what we take;
the larger kind we feel
for what we give.
~ Edwin Arlington
Robinson

"Blessed are those
that can give without
remembering and
receive without
forgetting.
~Author Unknown

Feeling gratitude
and not expressing it
is like wrapping
a present and
not giving it.
~William Arthur Ward

Giving

You say grace before meals. All right.
But I say grace before the concert and the opera,
and grace before the play and pantomime,
and grace before I open a book,
and grace before sketching, painting, swimming,
fencing, boxing, walking, playing, dancing
and grace before I dip the pen in the ink.
~G. K. Chesterton

Art

The essence of
all beautiful art,
all great art,
is gratitude.
~Friedrich Nietzsche

Gratitude is
an art of painting
an adversity
into a lovely picture.
~Kak Sri

IT IS IMPOSSIBLE *to feel grateful and depressed* IN THE SAME MOMENT

~NAOMI WILLIAMS

Hope

Gratitude is merely
the secret hope
of further favors.
~La Rochefoucauld

Hope has a
good memory,
gratitude a bad one.
~Baltasar Gracian

Sometimes
we should express
our gratitude
for the small and
simple things like
the scent of the rain,
the taste of your
favorite food,
or the sound of a loved
one's voice.
~Joseph B. Wirthlin

Attitude

There are moments
on most days
when I feel a deep
and sincere gratitude,
when I sit at the open
window, and there is
a blue sky.
~Käthe Kollwitz

For today
and its blessings,
I owe the world
an attitude
of gratitude.
~Clarence E. Hodges

Gratitude is the
best attitude.
~Author Unknown

Be grateful
for luck.
Pay the thunder
no mind –
listen to the birds.
And don't hate
nobody.
~Eubie

Happiness
cannot be traveled to,
owned, earned, worn or
consumed. Happiness is
the spiritual experience of
living every minute with
love, grace and gratitude.
~Denis Waitley

Happiness

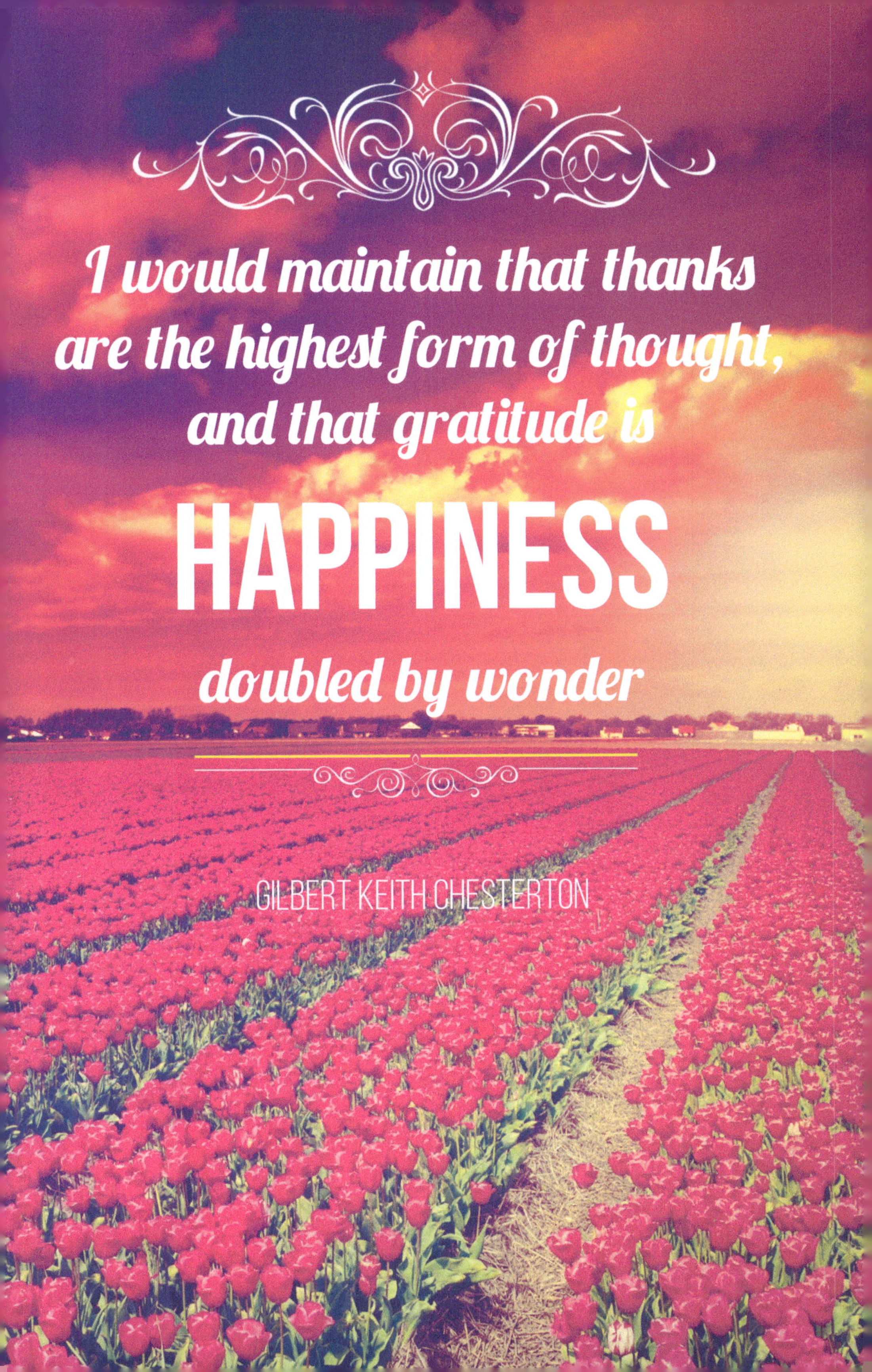

I would maintain that thanks are the highest form of thought, and that gratitude is

HAPPINESS

doubled by wonder

GILBERT KEITH CHESTERTON

Thanksgiving Day is a jewel, to set in the hearts of honest men; but be careful that you do not take the day, and leave out the gratitude.
~E.P. Powell

Thanksgiving Day comes, by statute, once a year; to the honest man it comes as frequently as the heart of gratitude will allow.
~Edward Sandford Martin

Thanksgiving

Thanksgiving was never meant to be shut up in a single day.
~Robert Caspar Lintner

Gratitude is the inward feeling of kindness received. Thankfulness is the natural impulse to express that feeling. Thanksgiving is the following of that impulse.
~Henry Van Dyke

GRATITUDE

is the sign of

NOBLE SOULS

~AESOP

Let us be
grateful to people
who make us happy
they are the
charming gardeners
who make
our souls blossom.
~Marcel Proust

Gratitude
is the fairest
blossom
which springs
from the soul.
~Henry Ward

If you
concentrate on finding
whatever is good
in every situation,
you will discover
that your life will suddenly
be filled with gratitude,
a feeling that
nurtures the soul.
~Rabbi Harold Kushner

Soul

Keeping
your body healthy
is an expression
of gratitude to the
whole cosmos –
the trees,
the clouds,
everything.
~Thich Nhat Hanh

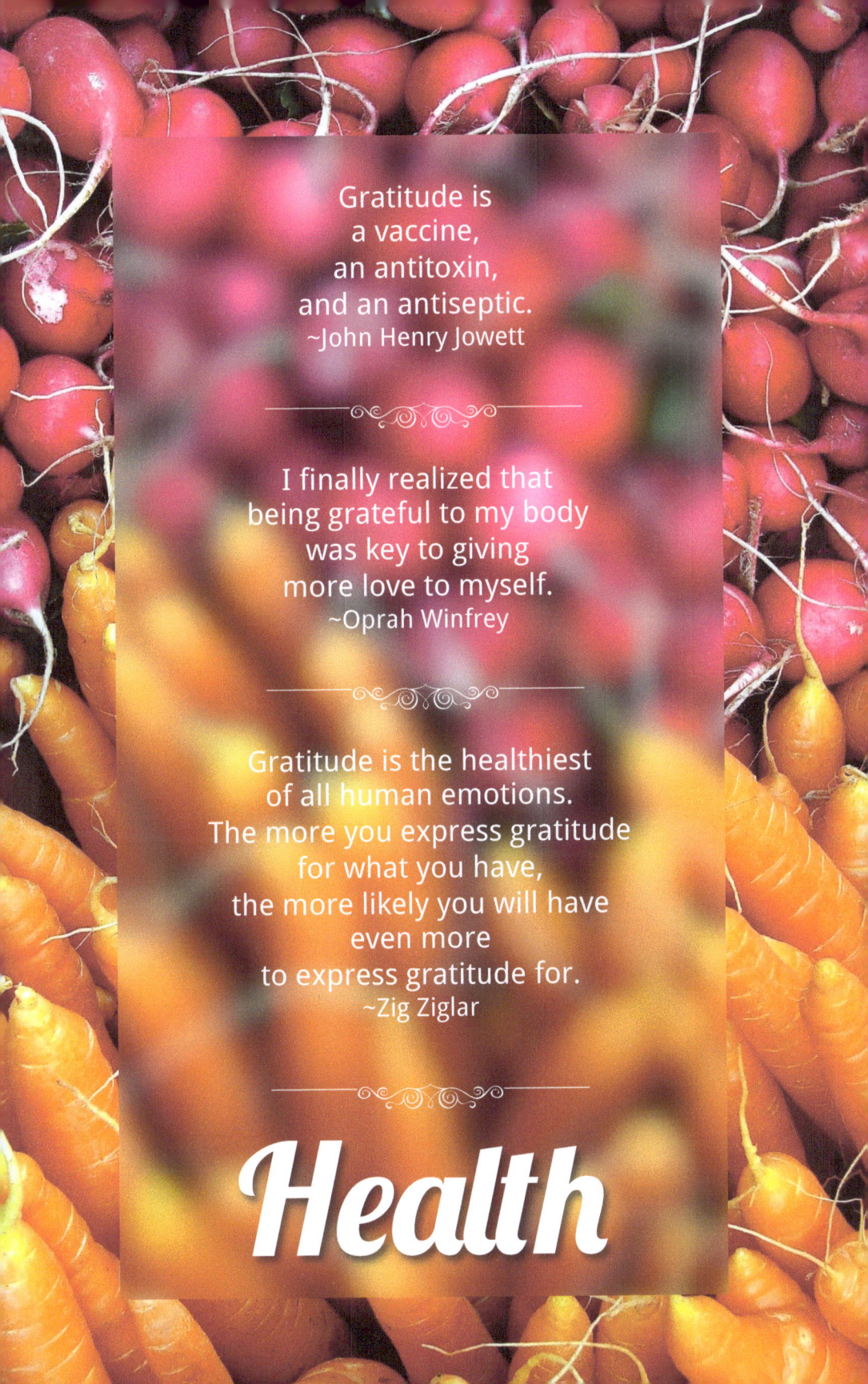

Gratitude is
a vaccine,
an antitoxin,
and an antiseptic.
~John Henry Jowett

I finally realized that
being grateful to my body
was key to giving
more love to myself.
~Oprah Winfrey

Gratitude is the healthiest
of all human emotions.
The more you express gratitude
for what you have,
the more likely you will have
even more
to express gratitude for.
~Zig Ziglar

Health

Gratitude
can transform
common days into
thanksgivings,
turn routine jobs
into joy, and change
ordinary opportunities
into blessings.
~William Arthur Ward

The discipline
of gratitude
is the explicit effort
to acknowledge
that all I am and have
is given to me
as a gift of love, a gift
to be celebrated
with joy.
~Henri Nouwen

Gratitude helps you
to grow and expand;
gratitude brings
joy and laughter
into your life and
into the lives of
all those around you.
~Eileen Caddy

Joy

God could not
be everywhere,
so he created mothers.
~Jewish Proverb

Mother

No gift to your mother can ever
equal her gift to you – life.
~Author Unknown

All that I am or ever hope to be,
I owe to my angel Mother.
~Abraham Lincoln

Mother's Day is in honor of the best
mother who ever lived –
The mother of your heart.
~Anna Jarvis

A mother is a person who seeing
there are only four pieces of pie
for five people, promptly announces
she never did care for pie.
~Tenneva Jordan

Gratitude
is the memory
of the heart.
~Jean Baptiste
Massieu

Gratitude is when memory is stored in the heart and not in the mind.
~Lionel Hampton

Gratitude is born in hearts that take time to count up past mercies.
~Charles E. Jefferson

There shall be eternal summer in the grateful heart.
~Celia Thaxter

When we focus on our gratitude, the tide of disappointment goes out and the tide of love rushes in.
~Kristin Armstrong

Heart

Gratitude
doesn't change the scenery.
It merely washes clean the glass
you look through so you can
clearly see the colors.
~Richelle E. Goodrich

Be grateful for all the
obstacles in your life. They
have strengthened you as you
continue with your journey.
~Author Unknown

We can always find something to be
thankful for, and there may be
reasons why we ought to be thankful
for even those dispensations which
appear dark and frowning.
~Albert Barnes

I am grateful for all my problems.
After each one was overcome, I became
stronger and more able to meet those
that were still to come.
I grew in all my difficulties.
~J. C. Penny

Challenges

Duty

Gratitude is a duty which ought to be paid, but which none have a right to expect.
~Jean-Jacques Rousseau

To the generous mind the heaviest debt is that of gratitude, when it is not in our power to repay it.
~Benjamin Franklin

The worst moment for an atheist is when he feels grateful and has no one to thank.
~Wendy Ward

Does not the gratitude of the dog put to shame any man who is ungrateful to his benefactors?
~Saint Basil

NO DUTY IS MORE
URGENT
THAN THAT OF
returning
THANKS

JAMES ALLEN

My Favorite Quotes
About Gratitude

My Favorite Quotes About Gratitude

FREE BONUS

As a thank you for buying this gratitude book,
I'm offering all readers my ebook
"Inspirational Picture Quotes about Friendship" for **FREE.**

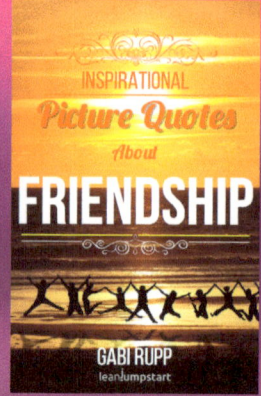

According to new research, true happiness lies in rewarding relationships,
not material wealth. Even if we as individuals can understand
the importance of close relationships on a social level,
some of us often forget that such relationships
are actually necessary for our own personal happiness.

You can download
"Inspirational Picture Quotes about Friendship" for FREE
by following the link below:

=> http://leanjumpstart.com/friendship7cs

OTHER BOOKS BY GABI RUPP IN THIS SERIES

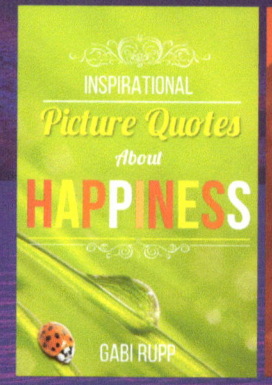
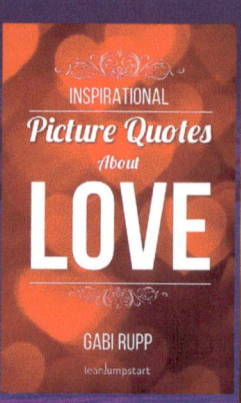

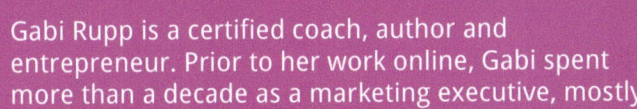

Gabi Rupp is a certified coach, author and entrepreneur. Prior to her work online, Gabi spent more than a decade as a marketing executive, mostly in the food and nutrition field, helping her clients realize their own projects. After her daughter was born, she found her true calling: writing, teaching, and coaching. Having the perfect life/work balance gave her the freedom to be a fulltime mother. In 2013 she founded leanjumpstart.com, where she uses a successful combination of proven science and practical experience to help people get in shape and stick with their new, healthy habits. Gabi is now happily settled in a little German town near the beautiful Black Forest region and spends her days with family, friends, and assisting clients as they overcome limitations and live life to its fullest potential.

Publisher: Gabi Rupp, Leanjumpstart.com /
gabi@leanjumpstart.com
Concept, Design & Layout: Gabi Rupp
Photo Credits: Footage Firm Inc., Dollar Photo Club ©:
altocumulus , apops, Austra, dfikar, Mat Hayward,
inmt , julenochek, george kuna, Francesco R
Iacomino, Marek, Monkey Business, petarpaunchev,
sommersprossen, sutsaiy , Tomsickova,
WavebreakMediaMicro, Lisa F. Young

1. Edition 2015
ISBN-13: 978-1512313918
ISBN-10: 1512313912